Leonard Bernstein
CANDIDE

LYRICS BY RICHARD WILBUR AND JOHN LATOUCHE
with additional lyrics by Leonard Bernstein and Lillian Hellman

ISBN 978-0-634-04674-2

LEONARD
BERNSTEIN
Music Publishing
Company LLC

BOOSEY & HAWKES

AN IMAGEM COMPANY

DISTRIBUTED BY

HAL•LEONARD®
CORPORATION
7777 W. BLUEMOUND RD. P.O. BOX 13819 MILWAUKEE, WI 53213

www.leonardbernstein.com
www.boosey.com
www.halleonard.com

LEONARD BERNSTEIN
August 25, 1918 - October 14, 1990

Leonard Bernstein was born in Lawrence, Massachusetts. He took piano lessons as a boy and attended the Garrison and Boston Latin Schools. At Harvard University he studied with Walter Piston, Edward Burlingame-Hill, and A. Tillman Merritt, among others. Before graduating in 1939 he made an unofficial conducting debut with his own incidental music to the Aristophanes play *The Birds*, and directed and performed in Marc Blitzstein's *The Cradle Will Rock*. Subsequently, at the Curtis Institute of Music in Philadelphia, Bernstein studied piano with Isabella Vengerova, conducting with Fritz Reiner, and orchestration with Randall Thompson.

In 1940 Bernstein studied at the Boston Symphony Orchestra's newly created summer institute, Tanglewood, with the orchestra's conductor, Serge Koussevitzky. Bernstein later became Koussevitzky's conducting assistant. He made a sensational conducting debut with the New York Philharmonic in 1943. Bernstein became Music Director of the orchestra in 1958. From then until 1969 he led more concerts with the orchestra than any previous conductor. He subsequently held the lifetime title of Laureate Conductor, making frequent guest appearances with the orchestra. More than half of Bernstein's 400-plus recordings were made with the New York Philharmonic.

Bernstein traveled the world as a conductor. Immediately after World War II, in 1946, he conducted in London and at the International Music Festival in Prague. In 1947 he conducted in Tel Aviv, beginning a relationship with Israel that lasted until his death. In 1953 Bernstein was the first American to conduct opera at the Teatro alla Scala in Milan, in Cherubini's *Medea* with Maria Callas.

Beyond many distinguished achievements as a composer of concert works, Bernstein also wrote a one-act opera, *Trouble in Tahiti* (1952), and its sequel, the opera *A Quiet Place* (1983). He collaborated with choreographer Jerome Robbins on three major ballets: *Fancy Free* (1944), and *Facsimile* (1946) for American Ballet Theater, and *Dybbuk* (1974) for the New York City Ballet. Bernstein composed the score for the award-winning film *On the Waterfront* (1954) and incidental music for the Broadway play *The Lark* (1955).

Bernstein contributed substantially to the Broadway musical stage. He collaborated with Betty Comden and Adolph Green on *On the Town* (1944) and *Wonderful Town* (1953). For *Peter Pan* (1950) he penned his own lyrics to songs and also composed incidental music. In collaboration with Richard Wilbur, Lillian Hellman and others he wrote *Candide* (1956). Other versions of *Candide* were written in association with Hugh Wheeler, Stephen Sondheim and other lyricists. In 1957 he collaborated with Jerome Robbins, Stephen Sondheim and Arthur Laurents on the landmark musical *West Side Story*, which was made into an Academy Award-winning film. Bernstein also wrote the Broadway musical *1600 Pennsylvania Avenue* (1976) with lyricist Alan Jay Lerner.

In 1985 the National Academy of Recording Arts and Sciences honored Bernstein with the Lifetime Achievement Grammy Award. He won eleven Emmy Awards in his career. His televised concert and lecture series were launched with the "Omnibus" program in 1954, followed by the extraordinary "Young People's Concerts with the New York Philharmonic," which began in 1958 and extended over fourteen seasons. Among his many appearances on the PBS series "Great Performances" was the acclaimed eleven-part "Bernstein's Beethoven." In 1989 Bernstein and others commemorated the 1939 invasion of Poland in a worldwide telecast from Warsaw.

Bernstein's writings were published in *The Joy of Music* (1959), *Leonard Bernstein's Young People's Concerts* (1961), *The Infinite Variety of Music* (1966), and *Findings* (1982). Each has been widely translated. He gave six lectures at Harvard University in 1972-1973 as the Charles Eliot Norton Professor of Poetry. These lectures were subsequently published and televised as *The Unanswered Question*.

Bernstein received many honors. He was elected in 1981 to the American Academy of Arts and Letters, which gave him its Gold Medal. The National Fellowship Award in 1985 applauded his life-long support of humanitarian causes. He received the MacDowell Colony's Gold Medal; medals from the Beethoven Society and the Mahler Gesellschaft; the Handel Medallion, New York City's highest honor for the arts; a Tony award (1969) for Distinguished Achievement in the Theater; and dozens of honorary degrees and awards from colleges and universities. Bernstein was presented ceremonial keys to the cities of Oslo, Vienna, Bersheeva, and the village of Bernstein, Austria, among others. National honors came from Italy, Israel, Mexico, Denmark, Germany (the Great Merit Cross), and France (Chevalier, Officer and Commandeur of the Legion d'Honneur). Bernstein received the Kennedy Center Honors in 1980.

In 1990 Bernstein received the Praemium Imperiale, an international prize created in 1988 by the Japan Arts Association and awarded for lifetime achievement in the arts. He used the $100,000 prize to establish initiatives in the arts and education, principally the Leonard Bernstein Center for Artful Learning.

Bernstein was the father of three children — Jamie, Alexander and Nina — and enjoyed the arrival of his first two grandchildren, Francisca and Evan.

TABLE OF CONTENTS

Notes on the Show and Songs

CANDIDE

Comic operetta in two acts. Original version withdrawn by the composer (not available for performance). Music by Leonard Bernstein. Book by Lillian Hellman (after Voltaire). Lyrics by Richard Wilbur, John LaTouche, Dorothy Parker, Lillian Hellman, Leonard Bernstein. First performance: October 29, 1956, Boston. Broadway opening: December 1, 1956. Directed by Tyrone Guthrie.

"Chelsea Version" 1973. Comic operetta in one act. Music by Leonard Bernstein. Book by Hugh Wheeler (after Voltaire). Lyrics by Richard Wilbur, John LaTouche, Stephen Sondheim, Leonard Bernstein. First performance: December 20, 1973, Chelsea Theater, Brooklyn, New York. Broadway opening: March 5, 1974. Directed by Harold Prince. John Mauceri, conductor.

"New York City Opera Version" 1982. Comic operetta in two acts. Music by Leonard Bernstein. Book by Hugh Wheeler (after Voltaire). Lyrics by Richard Wilbur, John LaTouche, Stephen Sondheim, Leonard Bernstein. First performance: October 13, 1982, New York City Opera.

"Scottish Opera Version" (revised Opera House version) 1988. Comic operetta in two acts. Music by Leonard Bernstein. Book by Hugh Wheeler (after Voltaire). Lyrics by Richard Wilbur, Stephen Sondheim, John LaTouche, Lillian Hellman, Dorothy Parker, Leonard Bernstein. First performance: May 17, 1988, Theatre Royal, Glasgow, Scotland. Edition by John Wells & John Mauceri (also conductor). Study score, vocal score, vocal selections, published by Boosey & Hawkes, for sale.

Oh, Happy We	**My Love**
It Must Be So	**Ballad of Eldorado**
Candide's Lament	**Words, Words, Words**
Dear Boy	**(Martin's Laughing Song)**
Glitter and Be Gay	**Bon Voyage**
You Were Dead, You Know	**Nothing More Than This**
I Am Easily Assimilated	**Make Our Garden Grow**

Candide has seen many versions over the years, receiving attention from renowned playwrights, lyricists and directors as it evolved through the years. In 1953, playwright Lillian Hellman proposed to Leonard Bernstein that they adapt Voltaire's *Candide* for the musical theatre. Voltaire's 18th-century novella satirized the fashionable philosophies of his day and, especially the Catholic church, whose Inquisition routinely tortured and killed "heretics" in a ghastly event known as an "Auto da Fé" ("act of faith" in medieval Spanish and Portuguese). Hellman observed a sinister parallel between the Inquisition's church-sponsored purges and the "Washington Witch Trials" being waged by the House Un-American Activities Committee against those suspected of communist ties. Fueled by rage and indignation, she began her adaptation of Voltaire's book. John LaTouche was engaged as initial lyricist, while Bernstein made numerous musical sketches. LaTouche (who died in 1956) was replaced by poet Richard Wilbur. Hellman, Bernstein and Wilbur worked periodically over the next two years, with concentrated attention to the project through 1956. By October, *Candide* was ready for performances in Boston. At some point during those Boston performances, Dorothy Parker contributed lyrics to "The Venice Gavotte," while Bernstein and Hellman had also added lyrics of their own to other numbers. The lyrics credits were already beginning to mount up.

The first Broadway production opened to mixed reviews, though the original recording sold well and Bernstein's score was highly valued. After a successful London opening in 1959, and other various productions in the United States, in 1973, Harold Prince (director), Hugh Wheeler (book author) and John Mauceri (conductor) devised a new, small-scale version with a revised book, with the support of Lillian Hellman, who at this time withdrew her original book adaptation of Voltaire. (The original 1956 version of *Candide* is a withdrawn work, no longer available for performance.) This new version, known as the "Chelsea Version" after the Brooklyn theatre where it had its try-out run, included additional lyrics by Stephen Sondheim, and a thirteen-instrument orchestration by Hershey Kay. Subsequently there was a New York City Opera version in 1982, with revised orchestrations by Bernstein, John Mauceri and Hershey Kay. The 1988 Scottish Opera production in Glasgow produced the final version of the show in

Bernstein's lifetime, which he conducted on the 1989 Deutsche Grammophon recording. The Scottish Opera Version is used in the published vocal score that is for sale. The "Chelsea Version" remains available on rental for more theatrical and less operatic productions.

A word of caution: There are some differences in the plot details in the various versions of *Candide*. Starting in Westphalia in Germany, described as "the best of all possible worlds," we meet Doctor Pangloss, philosopher and tutor to the virginal royal daughter Cunegonde, her beautiful brother Maximilian, the baron's bastard nephew Candide, and willing servant Paquette. After seeing the "gravitational experiment" Pangloss was teaching Paquette, chaste Cunegonde finds Candide to conduct the same experiment. A kiss leads them into the duet **"Oh, Happy We."** Caught investigating Cunegonde, Candide is thrown out of Westphalia, just as it is sacked and burned by the Bulgarian army, downcast as he sings **"It Must Be So."** They kill almost all but the gradually promiscuous Cunegonde, who is to be their concubine to survive. Candide believes her dead and sings his second meditation, **"Candide's Lament."** Distraught he runs into Pangloss, who tells him that Cunegonde's father and brother also are dead, and Pangloss's favorite Paquette. Pangloss sings **"Dear Boy"** in the face of adversity. (The chorus parts have been eliminated for this edition.)

Cunegonde is not dead, but escapes and hones her profession, and through a time-share agreement becomes the ornamented mistress of both a rich Jew and the Cardinal Archbishop of Paris. Cunegonde has developed a strong taste for the luxury given to her benefactors, apparent in **"Glitter and Be Gay,"** a witty spin on the operatic tradition of a "jewel song." She undresses for the evening as she sings, commenting on her "fallen state" while removing her finery and jewelry with the help of her maid servant, known simply as the Old Lady.

Surviving a shipwreck and a devastating volcano, Candide and Pangloss arrive in Lisbon just in time for the dreadful Auto da Fé. Candide and Cunegonde are amazed to find one another alive **("You Were Dead, You Know.")** Their reunion is short lived as Candide inadvertently kills Cunegonde's two masters. Cunegonde's companion, the Old Lady, joins them as they flee, pausing outside Cadiz, Spain. The Old Lady relates her many misfortunes, but attempts to help the situation by showing Candide and Cunegonde the art of adaptation in **"I Am Easily Assimilated"** (the chorus parts and Cunegonde's lines have been eliminated in this edition). The lovers and the Old Lady flee across the ocean to South America, where they come across Paquette and Maximilian, thought to be dead, now slaves to the Governor of Buenos Aires.

The Governor attempts to seduce Cunegonde and later Maximilian (dressed as a woman) in **"My Love."** ("My Love," a duet for the Governor and Cunegonde, has been adapted as a solo for this edition, cutting Cunegonde's lines. The Governor sings the song again a second time with Maximilian.) Maximilian is happy to hear from Candide that Cunegonde is alive, but is still enraged by bastard Candide's interest in his sister. Candide accidentally "kills" Maximilian (actually, he doesn't) and flees in the jungle with Paquette, only to stumble across Eldorado, a golden city of perfection **("Ballad of Eldorado,"** for Candide and chorus; chorus parts have been eliminated in this edition). Candide meets Martin, a miserable old Dutch roadsweeper. When Candide asks him if men of free will always will continue to massacre one another, Martin replies cynically with **"Words, Words, Words (Martin's Laughing Song)."** Candide tires of riches, and leaves to search for Cunegonde, who is now a courtesan to a rich Turk. Vanderdendur (acting for the Governor, who wants Candide's sheep and gold) sells Candide a boat full of holes in **"Bon Voyage."** (The song can also be sung by the Governor; "Bon Voyage" has been adapted for this edition, eliminating chorus parts and other adaptations.)

Candide and Paquette buy back Cunegonde and Maximilian (who miraculously is a slave in the household as well). Disappointed at the transformation of Cunegonde into purely a materialistic woman, Candide sings **"Nothing More Than This."** After some time in Venice the four seek out the Wisest Man in the World, who turns out to be Dr. Pangloss. He tells them that his new philosophy is to work hard, in rustic simplicity, for true perfection can never be achieved. All illusions are wiped away as the complete company sings of their new found moral clarity in **"Make Our Garden Grow."** (The principals are joined by a chorus in the show. All vocal parts are retained in this edition).

The selections from *Candide* in this collection use the published vocal score (Scottish Opera Version) as a source. From the vocal score, edited by Charles Harmon:

"This score incorporates the composer's final intentions regarding *Candide*. The engraving of this score is based on Leonard Bernstein's conducting score for his 1989 Deutsche Grammophon recording of *Candide*, as well as the orchestra material used in that recording, and the manuscripts of Leonard Bernstein at the Library of Congress."

Wednesday a.m.

Dear Lenny:

I send you the aria in its present condition, to show you that I have been working. Try this on your pianoforte.

A.)

Glitter and be gay,
That's the part I play:
I'm the toast of Paris, France —
Forced to bend my soul
To a sordid role,
Victimized by bitter, bitter circumstance.

Alas for me! Had I remained
Beside my lady mother,
My virtue had been kept unstained
Until my lily hand was gained
By some Grand Duke or other.

Ah, 'twas not to be;
Harsh necessity
Brought me to this gilded cage.
Born to higher things,
Here I droop my wings,
Singing of a sorrow nothing can assuage.

remained?

B.)

And yet of course I rather like to revel;
I have no strong objection to champagne;
My wardrobe is expensive as the devil;
Perhaps it is ignoble to complain.
Enough! Enough of being basely tearful!
I'll show my noble blood by being cheerful:

Facsimile of letter from Richard Wilbur to Leonard Bernstein including lyrics for "Glitter and Be Gay," additional notations by Leonard Bernstein

Facsimile of first page of composer's manuscript to "Glitter and Be Gay"

Facsimile of composer's manuscript to "Candide Continues His Travels/It Must Be Me"

Facsimile of composer's manuscript to "I Am Easily Assimilated"

Facsimile of composer's manuscript to "Make Our Garden Grow"

Foreword from the Published Vocal Score

Apropos Candide

Working with Lenny on *Candide*, I sometimes felt a certain territorial anxiety. I couldn't read or write music, but he could read books, played a mean game of anagrams, and was exceedingly quick and clever with words. I feared that I couldn't afford a writer's block, lest this very literate composer grow impatient and write my lyrics for me. Once, over luncheon with him and Lillian Hellman, I paraded my literacy by quoting some little-known lines from Lewis Carroll's *Sylvie and Bruno*; whereupon Lenny, to my distress, completed the quotation. But there was, on the whole, no need to be protective of my verbal domain; in our planning and making of numbers, Lenny did his best to rein in his versatility, and we had an agreeable division of labor.

Where we most collaborated on language was in the making of dummy lyrics, and that was always great fun. In cases where existing music was to be furnished with words, we often devised nonsensical verses which, embodying the music's rhythms in words of a sort, might bring me a little closer to the pertinent verbalizing of Lenny's sound and movement. On one occasion, for example, it occurred to us that a tune which Lenny had composed for the birthday of his son Alexander might serve for a number about Candide's departure from Buenos Aires in Act II. The tune – Lenny called it a species of *schottische* – was tripping and animated in the extreme, and it was therefore especially necessary for me to grope toward some verbal equivalent by way of a provisional or "dummy" lyric. The reader may be amused to know that the lyric of "Bon Voyage," in its dummy stage, began with these asinine lines:

> *Oh, what a lovely villager!*
> *Oh, what a lovely, lovely villager bird!*

People who question me about my work with Lenny are forever saying, "But you must have quarreled sometimes." Of course we did, though neither of us had an aptitude for stormy wrangling. I recall a day when, having differed about some number or other, we were sitting, mute and unhappy, in his studio at Lambert's Cove. After some minutes of silence, I began, quite unconsciously, to whistle. "Do you know what you're whistling?" Lenny exclaimed. "It's *'Pace, Pace'* from *Forza*! Oh," he went on, "how I envy that man's melodic inventiveness, and the way he could make something powerful out of the simplest jump-rope tune!" He moved to the piano and played Verdi's great aria, and before he was through we had quite forgotten ourselves, and our little differences, and were ready to get to work again.

Lenny's music for *Candide* seems to me perpetually fresh and exciting, and I am happy to have been part of an enterprise which prompted it.

Richard Wilbur
1993

Oh, Happy We

Duet for Soprano, Tenor

Lyrics by
RICHARD WILBUR

Music by
LEONARD BERNSTEIN

16

It Must Be So

Lyrics by
RICHARD WILBUR

Music by
LEONARD BERNSTEIN

Candide's Lament

Lyrics by
RICHARD WILBUR

Music by
LEONARD BERNSTEIN

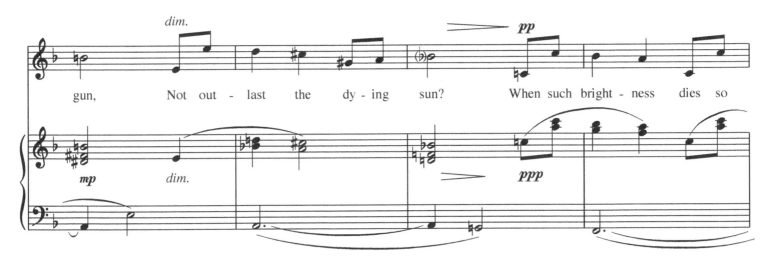

moon.   Good-bye, my love, my love, good - bye.   Good-bye, my love, my love, good-

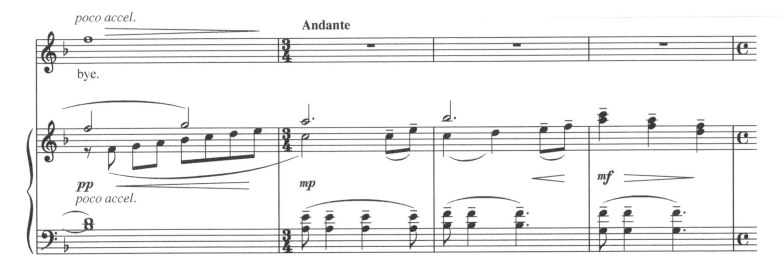

bye.

Cu-ne-gon - de!   Cu-ne-gon - de!

Dear Boy

Lyrics by
RICHARD WILBUR

Music by
LEONARD BERNSTEIN

did the deed, Through Na-ture's gen-tle laws, And how should ill ef-
versed the seas And come in-fect-ed back, Why, think of all the
vent the spread Of Love's di-vine dis-ease; It rounds the world from

fects pro-ceed From so di-vine a cause? Dear boy:
lux-u-ries That mod-ern life would lack! Dear boy:
bed to bed As pret-ty as you please. Dear boy:

Andantino (Tempo I tranquillo)

Sweet hon-ey comes from bees that sting, As you are well a-ware; To
All bit-ter things con-duce to sweet, As this ex-am-ple shows; With-
Men wor-ship Ve-nus ev-'ry-where, As may be plain-ly seen; Her

one a-dept in rea-son-ing, What ev-er pains dis-
out the lit-tle spi-ro-chete, We'd have no choc-o-
dec-o-ra-tions which I bear Are no-bler than the

Glitter and Be Gay

Lyrics by
RICHARD WILBUR

Music by
LEONARD BERNSTEIN

Tempo di Valse Lente

CUNEGONDE:

Glit-ter and be gay, That's the part I play:

Here I am in Par - is, France.

Forced to bend my soul To a sor-did role,

Vic-tim-ized by bit - ter, _____ bit - ter cir-cum-stance. A -

Un poco animato   **rall.**

las   for me! ___ Had I   re-mained   Be-side my   la-dy mo-ther, My

a tempo   *cresc.*   **rall.**

vir - tue had ___ re-mained   un-stained   Un-til my   maid-en hand   was

28

dev - il, ha ha! Per - haps it is ig - no - ble to com -

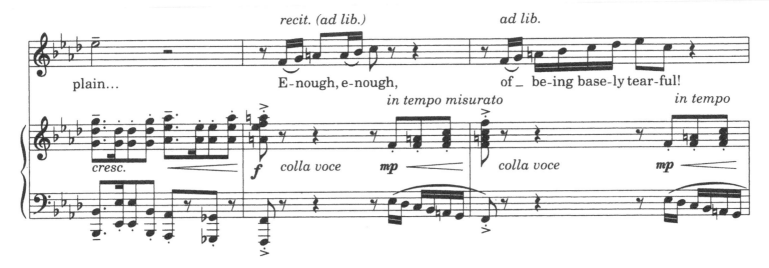

plain... E-nough, e-nough, of _ be-ing base-ly tear-ful!

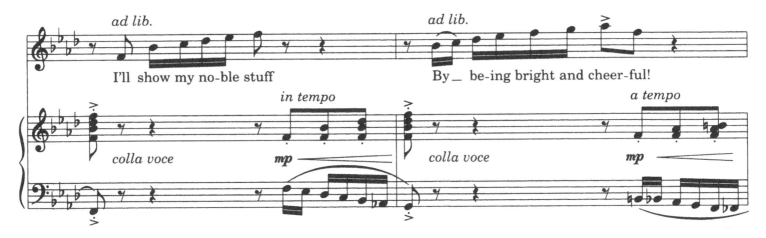

I'll show my no-ble stuff By _ be-ing bright and cheer-ful!

Ha ha ha ha ha! Ha! _____

(she begins to remove her jewelry and hand it over to the Old Lady)

Ha ha ha ha ha ha! Ha ha ha ha ha — ha ha ha! Ha ha ha ha ha ha!

Ha ha ha ha ha — ha ha ha! Ha ha ha ha ha ha! Ha ha ha ha ha — ha ha

ha! Ha ha ha ha ha ha! Ha ha ha ha ha ha! Ha ha ha ha

ha ha ha ha ha ha! Ha ha ha ha ha ha ha

ha! Ha ha ha ha ha ha! Ha ha ha ha ha
ha! Ha _____ ha!

ha! Ha _____ ha _____
Ha _____ ha _____ ha _ ha _ ha _ ha! _____

ad lib. (like a sigh)

Tempo primo (sobs)   **rall.**   **Meno mosso**
(she continues removing her jewelry)

(parlando) Pearls   Ah, how can
and ruby rings...   wordly things

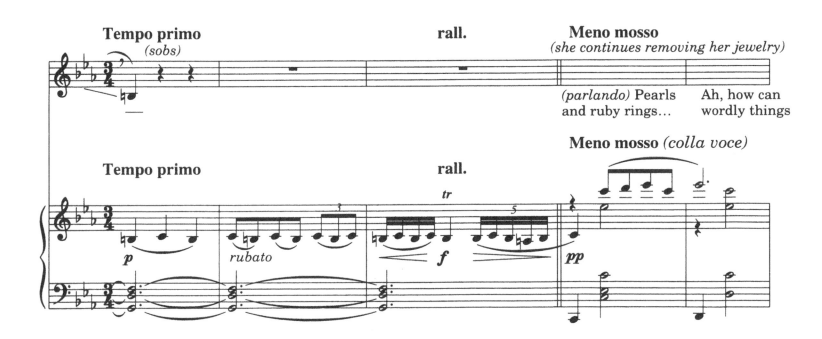

Take the place of Honor lost?   Can they compensate For my fallen state,   Purchased as they were

at such an awful cost?   Bracelets...lavallieres...   Can they dry   Can they blind
                                                           my tears?

my eyes to shame? Can the brightest brooch Shield me from reproach? Can the purest diamond purify my

Allegro molto, come prima

name?   And yet,   of course, these trin - kets are en - dear-ing,   ha ha!   I'm

Allegro molto, come prima

oh, so glad my sap - phire is a star, ha ha! ____ I

rath - er like a twen - ty car - at ear - ring, ha ha! If

quasi parlando

I'm not pure, at least my jew-els are! E-nough, e-nough!

recit. (ad lib.)

in tempo misurato

colla voce

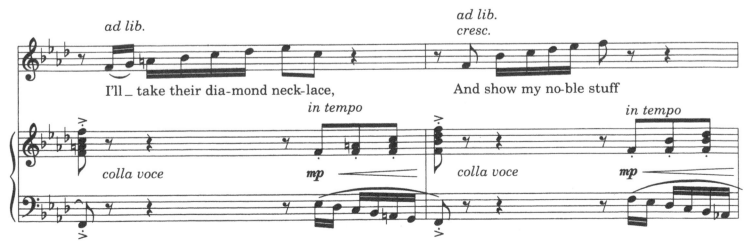

I'll _ take their dia-mond neck-lace, And show my no-ble stuff

ad lib. *ad lib.* *cresc.*

in tempo *in tempo*

colla voce *colla voce*

By — be-ing gay and reck-less! Ha ha ha ha ha!

Ha! _____ Ha ha ha ha ha ha!

(the jewelry gone, she begins

to undress)

Ha ha ha ha ha — ha ha ha! Ha ha ha ha ha ha! Ha ha ha ha ha — ha ha ha!

Ha ha ha ha ha ha! Ha ha ha ha ha — ha ha ha! Ha ha ha ha ha

35

ha! Ha ha ha ha ha ha! Ha ha ha ha ha ha ha ha ha ha!

Un poco più mosso

Ha ha ha ha ha ha ha Ha! Ob-serve how brave-ly I con -

ceal The_ dread-ful, drea-(hea)d-ful shame I _ feel. Ha ha ha ha! Ha ha ha ha! Ha

ha ha ha! Ha ha ha ha! Ha ha ha ha! _____ Ha ha ha ha! Ha_ ha ha

Ossia ha! Ha _ ha ha _

* Downbeat may be omitted in soprano.

You Were Dead, You Know

Duet for Soprano, Tenor

Lyrics by
JOHN LATOUCHE

Music by
LEONARD BERNSTEIN

CUNEGONDE: *mp grazioso*

That is ver-y true. Ah, but love will find a way.

too. Then what

We'll go in-to that an-oth-er day. Now let's talk of you.

did you do?

You are look-ing ver-y well. Weren't you clev-er, dear, to sur-vive?

I've a sor-ry tale to

Love of mine, where did you tell; I es-caped more dead than a-live.

go? Oh, what tor-ture, oh, what pain...
Oh, I wan-dered to and fro... Hol-land, Por-tu-gal and

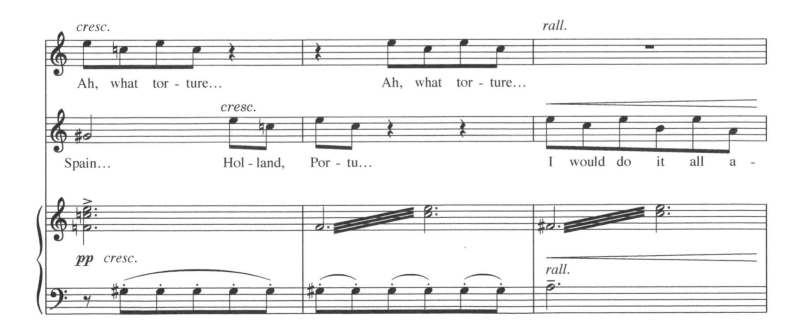

Ah, what tor-ture... Ah, what tor-ture...
Spain... Hol-land, Por-tu... I would do it all a-

(they waltz with abandon around the room)

I Am Easily Assimilated

Music and Lyrics by
LEONARD BERNSTEIN

The song is for the Old Lady, Cunegonde, Two Señores and chorus, adapted as a solo for this edition.

Di dee di! Dee di dee di! I am eas-i-ly as-sim-i-la-ted.
Por fa-vor! To-re-a-dor! I am eas-i-ly as-sim-i-la-ted.

I am so eas-i-ly as-sim-i-la-ted.
I am so eas-i-ly as-sim-i-la-ted.

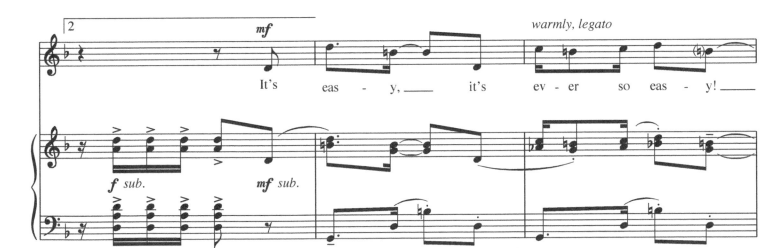

It's eas-y,___ it's ev-er so eas-y!___

I'm Span-ish,___ I'm

sud-den - ly Span - ish! ___ And you must be Span-ish, too.

Do like the na - tives do. These days you have to be In the ma -

jor - i - ty.

Mís

la - bios _ ru - bí, Drei - vier - tel Takt, mon très cher a - mi, _____ Oui oui, sí

dolce

sí, ja ja ja, yes yes, _ da da. Je ne sais quoi! _____

mf   *mp*

mf cresc.

A

long way _ from Rov - no Gu - ber - nya! _____

ff

Mís

cresc.

48

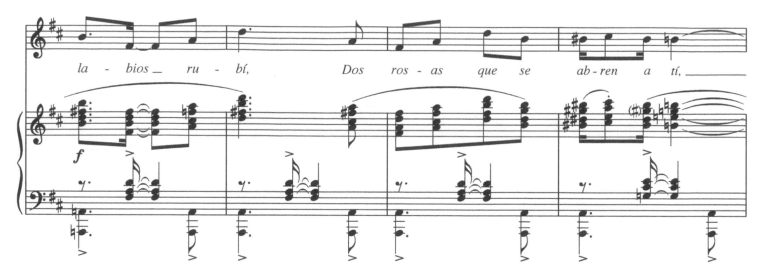

la - bios _ ru - bí, Dos ros - as que se ab - ren a tí, ____

____ Con - quis - tan tu co - ra - zón, Y só - lo con U - na di - vi - na can - ción ____

____ De mís la - bios ru - bí! ____ Ru - - bí! ____

cresc.

____ Ru - bí! _____ Hey!

My Love
(Governor's Serenade)

Lyrics by
RICHARD WILBUR and JOHN LATOUCHE

Music by
LEONARD BERNSTEIN

For the original duet version of this song for the Governor and Cunegonde, see the *Candide* vocal score.

50

bless - ing. Just a week in bed, And we'll be con - va -

lesc - ing. Why talk of mor - als When spring - time is

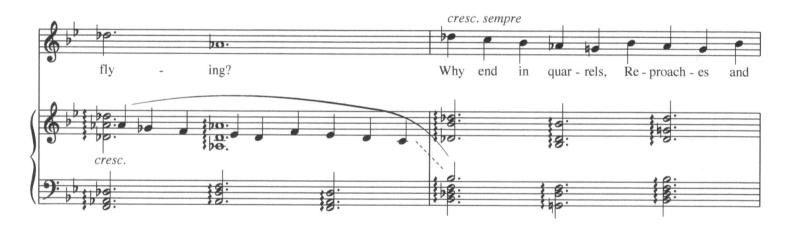

fly - ing? Why end in quar - rels, Re - proach - es and

sigh - ing, Cry - ing for love? ___ My love? ___ Well,

Since you're so pure, I shall be - troth you, my love, Though I feel sure I'll come to

loathe you, my love. Still for the thrill I'm per - fect - ly will - ing. _____ For

if we must wed _____ Be - fore we may bed, _____ Then come let us wed, _____ my

love! _____

Ballad of Eldorado

Lyrics by
LILLIAN HELLMAN

Music by
LEONARD BERNSTEIN

The song is for Candide and chorus; chorus has been eliminated for this edition.

down a prim-rose moun-tain, A - cross a sea-shell sea, To a

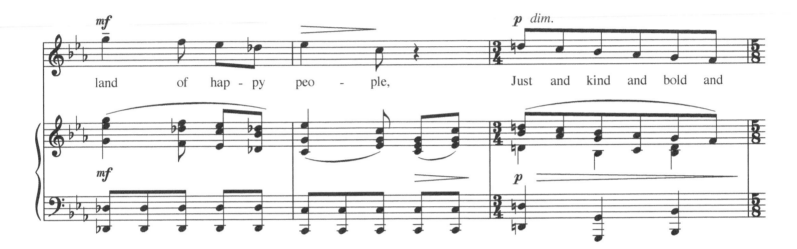

land of hap-py peo - ple, Just and kind and bold and

free. _____ They

1. bathe each dawn in a gold-en lake, Em-'ralds hang up -
2. gave me home, they called me friend, They taught me how to

54

on the vine. / All is there for all to take,
live in grace. / Sea - sons passed with - out an end

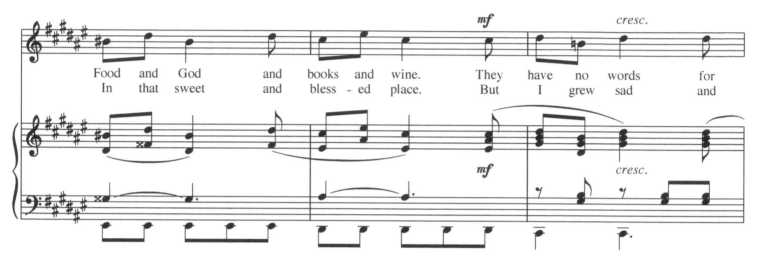

Food and God and books and wine. / They have no words for
In that sweet and and bless - ed place. / But I grew sad for and

fear and greed, / For lies and war, re - venge and rage. / They
could not stay; / With - out my love my heart grew cold, / So they

sing and dance and think and read / They live in peace and
sad - ly sent me on my way / With gra - cious gifts and of

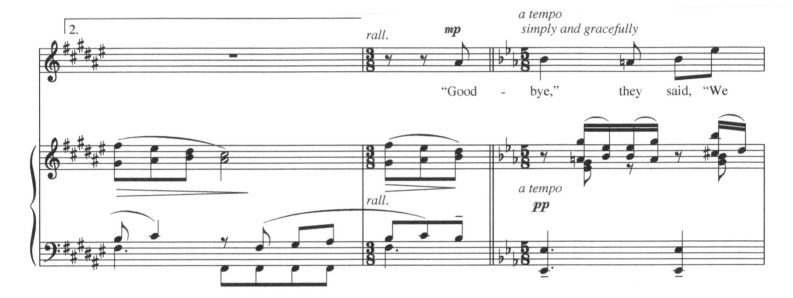

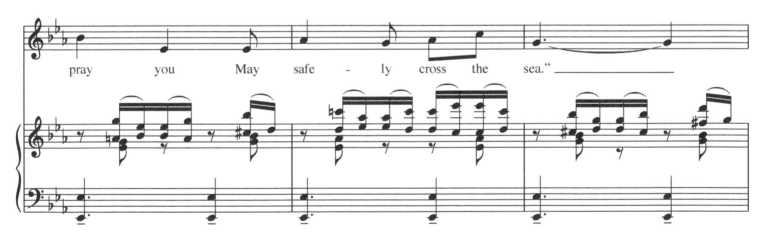

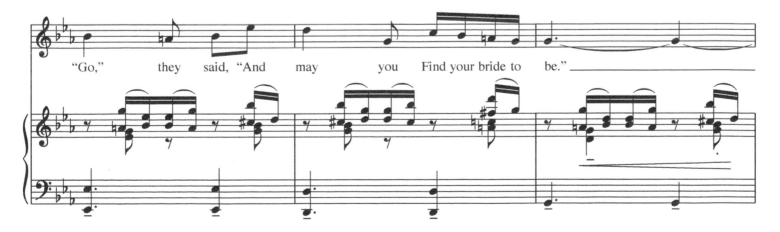

die of age.
gems and gold.

They

"Good - bye," they said, "We

pray you May safe - ly cross the sea." _____

"Go," they said, "And may you Find your bride to be." _____

55

Then past the jun - gle foun - tain, A - long a sil - ver

shore, I've come by sea and moun - tain, to be with my love once

more. _____ To be with my love once

more. _____

Words, Words, Words
(Martin's Laughing Song)

Music and Lyrics by
LEONARD BERNSTEIN

Tempo di Bolero
(Allegro marcato)

MARTIN:

(almost laughing)

f (carried away)

Ha ha ha ha,   ha ha ha ha   ha ha ha ha ha!

mp   *cresc.*   *f*

1. Words, words, words, words,   I   have   no   words
2. 'Mid   grime   and   slime   Why   waste   our   time

p sub.

To de-scribe the van - i - ty of life,   The in - sane in - an - i - ty of life,
Spout-ing some Spi - no - za mon - o-graph,   E - ven one short Shake-speare ep - i-taph.

cresc.

cresc.

f

1.

I   have   no   words,   but   ha!
They   make   me   laugh,   but

mf   *f*   *p*

wait! There just oc - curred to me, A word _____ that may just pos - si - bly

Ap - ply to all of us Trapped on this ball of dust.

Two ti - ny syl - la - bles but spi - ny syl - la - bles;

One sin - gle word: ab - surd. Ha! Ab - surd. Ha! Ab -

60

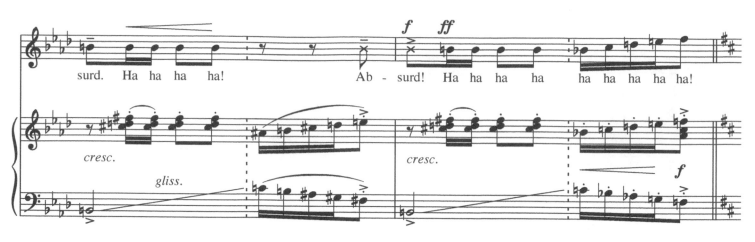

surd. Ha ha ha ha!   Ab - surd! Ha ha ha ha ha ha ha ha ha!

(gasp)   *(groaning)*

Don't make me laugh,   It hurts to laugh!   Oh, __ oh, __

(in pain)

__ Whoa, ho, ho, ho, ho, ho!   Don't make me laugh!

Don't make me tit - ter! All wheat is chaff, All pills are bit - ter.

No-thing to trust in This worst of all pos - si - ble worlds. All ends in

dust in This worst of all pos - si - ble worlds. An - y ques - tions?

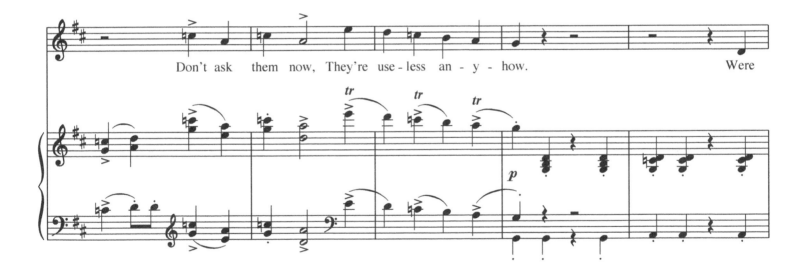

Don't ask them now, They're use-less an - y - how. Were

you in my po - si - tion, friend, Were you a hum - ble sweep - er, Your

thoughts on man's con - di - tion, friend, Would be a lit - tle deep - er. If

ev - 'ry bles - sed day, my friend, Brought dung and bone and spit - tle For

you to clear a - way, my friend 'Twould change your mind a lit - tle. Yes,

dung and bone and spit - tle And mud and trash And blood and ash And

souvenirs of lust ____ And ev-'ry sort of res-i-due In

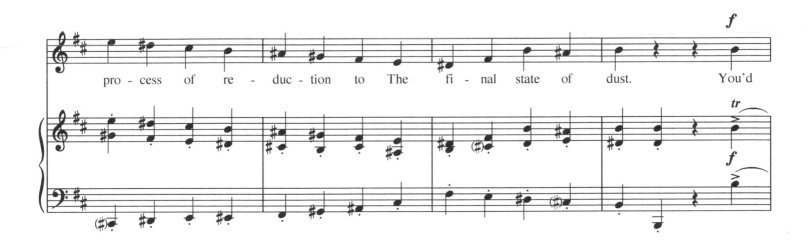

pro-cess of re-duc-tion to The fi-nal state of dust. You'd

laugh a-long with me, my friend, You'd laugh un-til you'd

bust! Hah! Ha ha ha ha

(takes three bars to recover his dour Martinship)

ha ha ha ha ha ha ha ha ha!

Huh.

(nasty) Heh. *(disgusted)* Pphff. *(resigned)* Tchhh.

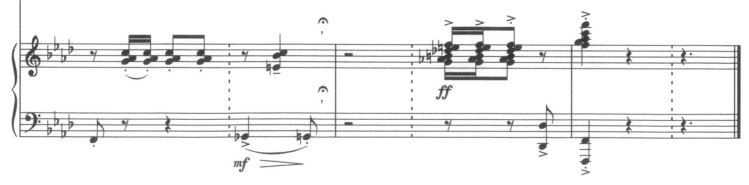

(taunting) Nyaah. *(wild)* Ha!!

Bon Voyage

Lyrics by
RICHARD WILBUR

Music by
LEONARD BERNSTEIN

Chorus has been cut from this solo edition, among other adaptations.

66

Oh, but I'm bad. Oh, but I'm bad, Play-ing such a ver-y dirt-y trick on

such a fine lad! I'm a low cad, I'm a low cad, Al-ways when I do this sort of thing it

makes me so sad, Ev-er so sad! Oh, but I'm bad! Ev-er so bad!

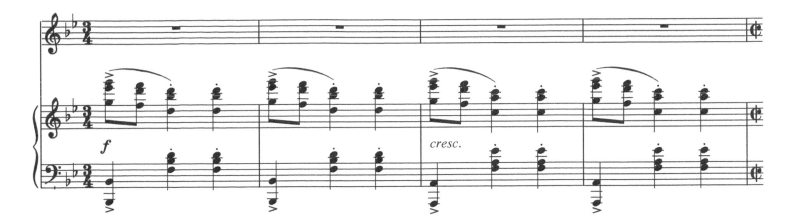

Bon _____ voy - age. I'm so

rich that my life is an ut - ter bore; There is just not a thing that I

need. My de - sires are as dry as an ap - ple core, And my

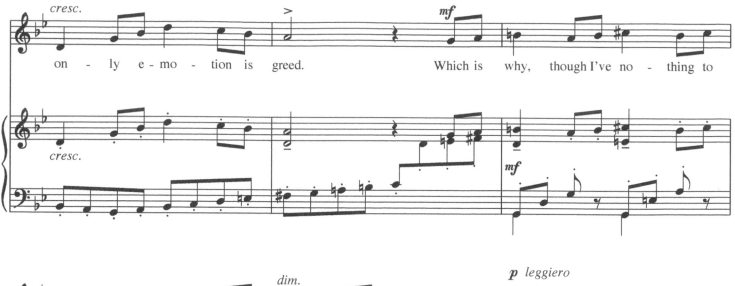

on - ly e - mo - tion is greed. Which is why, though I've no - thing to

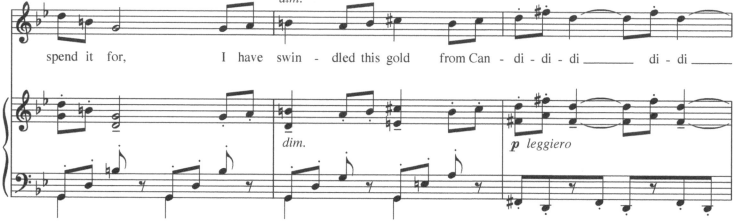

spend it for, I have swin - dled this gold from Can - di - di - di _____ di - di _____

_____ di - di - di - di - di - di - di - di - di - dide, Poor Can - dide! But I

nev - er would swin - dle the hum - ble poor, For you can't get a tur - nip to

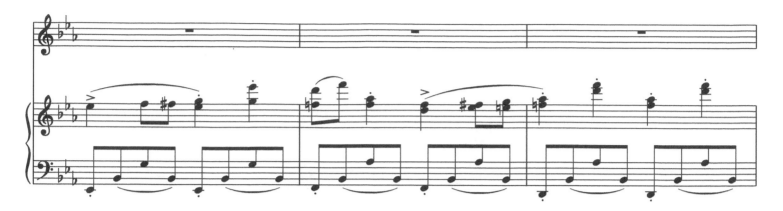

What a dumb goat, what a dumb goat, Hand-ing me a

for - tune for a per - fect wreck of a boat. Nev - er did float, nev - er

did float. This is going to make a most a - mus - ing an - ec - dote. Nev - er

did float, wreck of a boat, What a dumb goat!

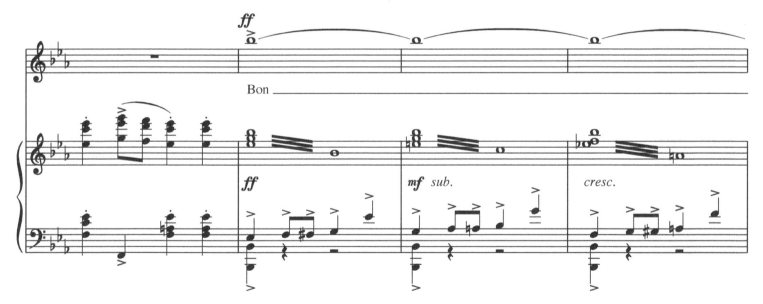

Bon

voy - age!!

Nothing More Than This

Music and Lyrics by
LEONARD BERNSTEIN

Make Our Garden Grow

Lyrics by
RICHARD WILBUR

Music by
LEONARD BERNSTEIN

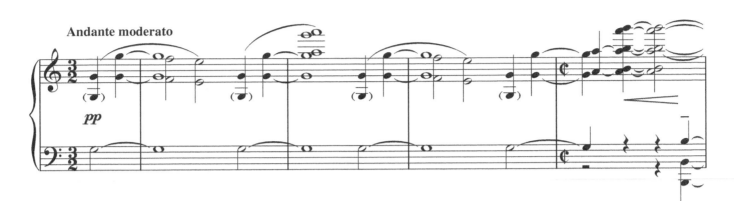

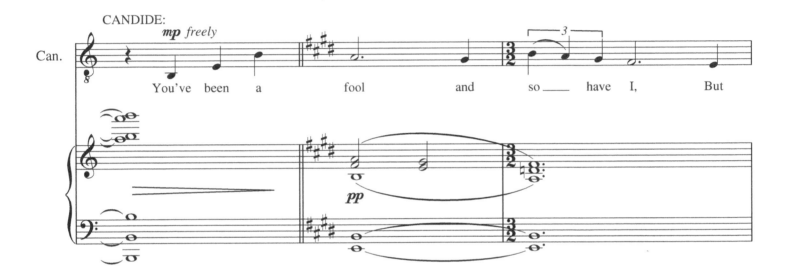

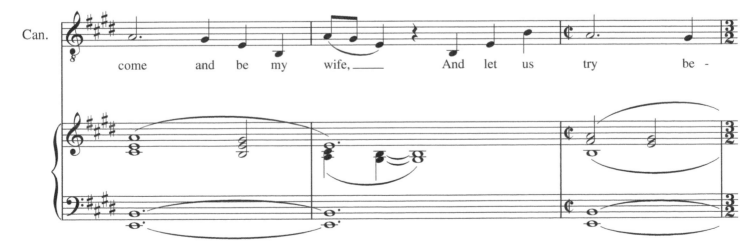

76

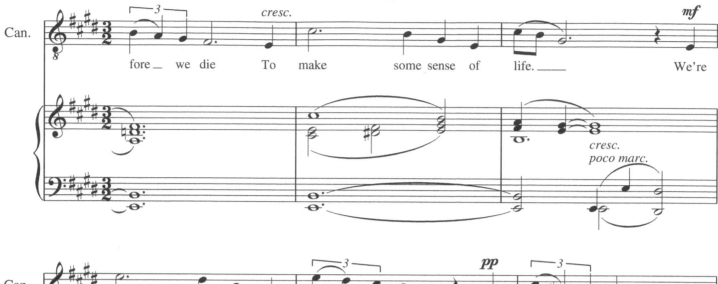

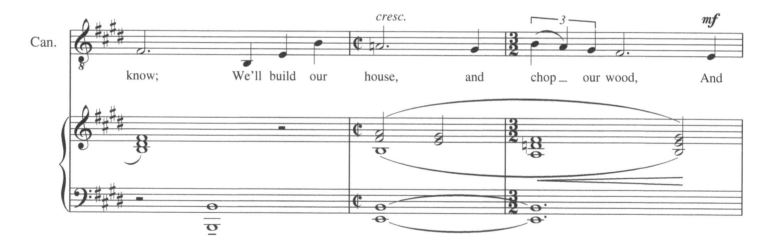

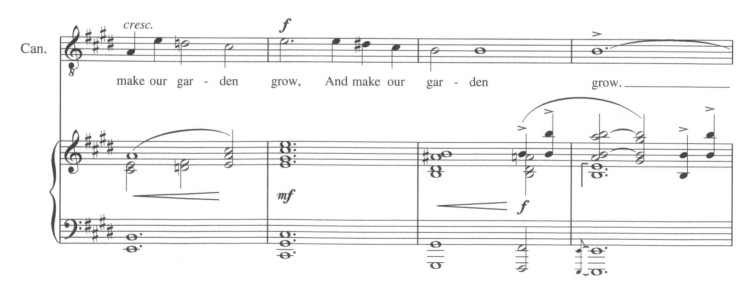

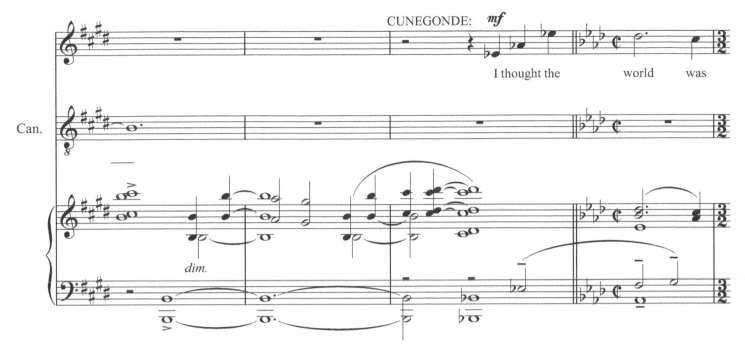

CUNEGONDE: *mf*

I thought the world was

sug - ar - cake, For so our mas - ter said; ___ But now I'll

teach my hands _ to bake Our loaf of dai - ly bread. _ We're

CANDIDE: *f*

We're

78

80

84

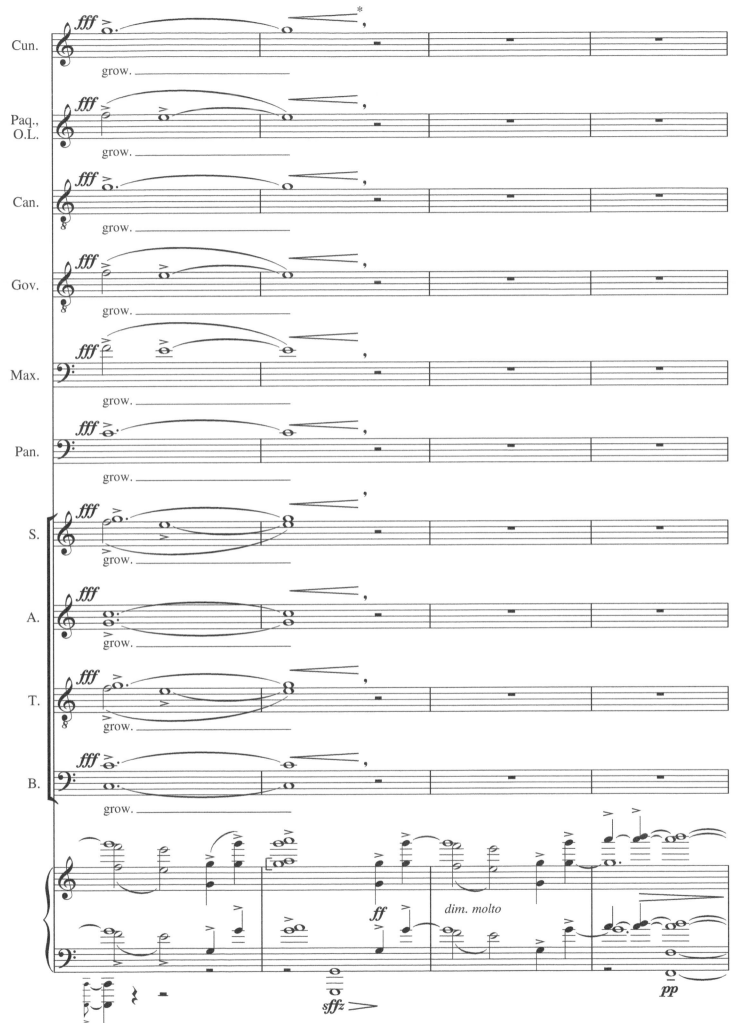

*In the 1956 production a cut was made from the middle of bar 64 to the middle of bar 67.